WITHDRAWN

High School for Performing
and Visual Arts
Houston, Texas

Presented by:

PAT ZEITOUN

THE NATIONAL POETRY SERIES

Seventh Annual Series—1986

Lynn Doyle, *Living Gloves* (Selected by Cynthia Macdonald)

Stephen Dunn, *Local Time* (Selected by Dave Smith)

Alice Fulton, *Palladium* (Selected by Mark Strand)

Reginald Gibbons, *Saints* (Selected by Roland Flint)

Jack Meyers, *As Long as You're Happy* (Selected by Seamus Heaney)

The National Poetry Series was established in 1978 to publish five collections of poetry annually through five participating publishers. The manuscripts are selected by five poets of national reputation. Publication is funded by James A. Michener, Edward J. Piszek, The Ford Foundation, Mobil Foundation, Exxon Corporation, Friends of the National Poetry Series, The National Endowment for the Arts, and the five publishers—E. P. Dutton, Graywolf Press, William Morrow & Co., Persea Books, and the University of Illinois Press.

LIVING GLOVES

For Pat Zeitoun,
with great affection,

Lynn Doyle
Sept 26, 1986

Lynn Doyle

LIVING GLOVES

The National Poetry Series · Selected by Cynthia Macdonald

811.54
Doy

E. P. DUTTON · NEW YORK

Copyright © 1986 by Lynn Doyle
All rights reserved. Printed in the U.S.A.
  Parts of "Dexterity" are taken from The Complete Letters
of Vincent van Gogh, Vol. 3, New York Graphic Society:
Greenwich, Connecticut, 1958.
  "My Mother in Majorca" was published in Shenandoah.
"The Good Hands People Know Their Bodies," "Wake Up," and
"Negotiated Settlements and Immediate Withdrawals"
were published in Poetry Northwest.
"Friday Nights on the Floor" and
"Summer Resort" were published in Domestic Crude. *Some of these*
poems were first published in a slightly different form.

No part of this publication may be reproduced or transmitted
in any form or by any means, electronic or mechanical, including
photocopy, recording, or any information storage and retrieval
system now known or to be invented, without permission in
writing from the publisher, except by a reviewer who wishes to
quote brief passages in connection with a review written for
inclusion in a magazine, newspaper, or broadcast.

Published in the United States by
E. P. Dutton, a division of New American Library,
2 Park Avenue, New York, N.Y. 10016.

Library of Congress Cataloging-in-Publication Data
Doyle, Lynn.
Living gloves.
(The National poetry series)
I. Title. II. Series.
PS3554.O9747L5 1986   811'.54   85-27545

ISBN: 0-525-24416-6 (cloth)
       0-525-48215-6 (paper)

Published simultaneously in Canada
by Fitzhenry & Whiteside Ltd., Toronto

Designed by Steven N. Stathakis

10 9 8 7 6 5 4 3 2 1

First Edition

*For George Klein,
in sickness and in health
1960–1986*

I wish to thank my family for their unending love and generous support over these many years. I could not have completed this book without them. Special thanks also to Winifred Claggett and Joseph Schoolar for their faith in me, and to Cynthia Macdonald, Charles Wright, and Gregory Orr for their careful, supportive criticism of my work.

CONTENTS

I.

MY MOTHER IN MAJORCA   2
THE GOOD HANDS PEOPLE KNOW
    THEIR BODIES   4
WONDER   6
FRIDAY NIGHTS ON THE FLOOR   8
PYROKINESIS   11
I PICK OUT CLOTHES FOR MY MOTHER   14
NEGOTIATED SETTLEMENTS AND IMMEDIATE
    WITHDRAWALS   16
SUMMER RESORT   18
DEXTERITY   19
PATIENCE MUFFET   22

II.

MIAMI   26

THE TAKING OFF OF NIGHTGOWNS AND THE
    REMOVING OF BANDAGES   28

LIVING GLOVES   30

BEARING   32

VACATIONS AND JUSTIFIABLE CAUSES   35

MASH   37

EARTH   39

HINDSIGHT   42

UNCLE WALTER   44

LIP SERVICE   46

III.

GEORGE   52

NECK AND NECK AND NECK OR NOTHING   56

THE EMBARRASSMENT   57

SCHOOL OF THE WOODS   58

WAKE UP   60

*This symbol is used to indicate a break in the stanza of a poem wherever a stanza is interrupted because of pagination.

I

MY MOTHER IN MAJORCA

My mother in Majorca for the summer writes a letter.

In Majorca, it's sun, hot and dry, cracking sun.
In Majorca, it's rock, jagged and orcharded, olive rock.
In Majorca, it's sea, mirroring and clear, isolating sea.
Take it from me, I'm having a great time.

My mother in Majorca searches for bodies.
A mountain fell there Before Christ, a landslide.
My mother in Majorca searches for survivors.

In Majorca, the expedition found a necklace.
In Majorca, we dig and sift, shovel and scrape.
Take it from me, there are four layers left to go.

My mother in Majorca glues and pieces a people together.

In Majorca, we found an oven and some shards.
In Majorca, the women bear, cook and clean, and bear, then die.

*

> *Take it from me, your father expects a tight house.*
> *Take it from me, change the sheets on Mondays.*

My mother in Majorca imagines life.

> *In Majorca, they bury their dead with lime.*
> *In Majorca, people eat seafood and fruit, seafood and snails and olives.*
> *In Majorca, people drink.*
> *Take it from me, your brother needs food to grow.*
> *Take it from me, your father is nasty after a beer.*

My mother in Majorca catalogues.

> *In Majorca, Robert Graves walks into Deya to get his mail.*
> *In Majorca, we sit in cafés late and talk, sit and talk.*
> *Take it from me, your father comes home at eight.*
> *Take it from me, your father needs attention.*

My mother in Majorca compares two cultures.

> *In Majorca, people make coffee without filters.*
> *In Majorca, children grow up in spite of parents.*
> *Take it from me, these people never heard of Adler.*

My mother in Majorca searches for survivors.
A depression ruptured the family in Houston, a rift.
My mother in Majorca writes home.

> *In Majorca, a Hilton is in Palma, a Hilton and other resorts.*
> *In Majorca, they sell jewelry and coral, jewelry and olive-wood bowls.*
> *In Majorca, the international papers are flown in daily.*
> *Take it from me, I'm having a great time.*

My mother in Majorca brings home her island.

3

THE GOOD HANDS PEOPLE KNOW THEIR BODIES

Solo violinists say how natural it is to play
with the chin rested and both arms above
the diaphragm level. They bellow their backs
in order to breathe, extending and arcing
in a manner fitting a concertina.
It is when inexperienced lungs wait
for breaks in fingering or sudden downbeat
strokes that their toes go into spasm,
the feet wanting to leave the floor.

French bakers say always check for bunions
before ordering fine breads and pastries.
The time it takes to learn rolling,
be able to change a dust bowl of clouds
into a sky of croissants, is exactly one bunion.
And the madness that follows, the rolling
well into the middle of the night
and the compensating, the eating of what doesn't rise
like indiscriminate ladyfingers, is the second.

Prostitutes say that underneath all the panting
and promising, they are not even near there at all.
Really they are remembering a sister's birthday
or making a grocery list of orange juice and jelly.
Letting the body feel something is the lowest form
of infidelity, like a shrink jacking off behind the desk.
It's not part of the money. It's not part of the habit.
Sometimes, depending upon the person and the price,
it's not even faithful to think.

Some people believe in the power of Jesus,
say they have the ability to straighten backs
with the touch of their hands. Years of pain and anguish
vanish completely in a matter of seconds. But most clergy
confess simply that the way to be saved is not easy.
It must be done bit by bit, deed by deed, over and over.
God pays off for the labors of love. The bigger
the virtue, the higher the premium. But the effort
is yours. You will soon be what you are now becoming.

Coroners report that no body is unremarkable.
Sometimes in suicides, they'll find advanced syphilis,
impending appendicitis, or right-sided hearts.
Even in plane crashes it is possible to tell
where most arms and legs go, their patterns leaving
a permanent impression. Some bodies, drifters,
refuse recognition, must be kept the entire shelf life,
until their bones settle down, assume a posture
long enough to be noticed.

WONDER

for Sharon Claggett Nicholson

It's heavenly, the smell of fresh bread
five blocks up at Wonder, like Grandmother's
kitchen or the French Gourmet Bakery.
Even Tommy, when he comes home
from work, smells of Brown 'n Serve.
But he won't let me kiss him until after
he's showered and shaved it off
with Old Spice. Dinner is no better.
Back in Omaha, used to be we ate
a dozen Pull-Aparts or at least
three Mini-Loafs in one sitting.
Now, well, dinner might as well be meatless
without that touch of yeast.
Since he's got that job racking,
and even cinnamon rolls are free,
he says he hates the stuff and tells me
of dough fights with mixers and the sweat
from fat men dripping into vats.
He'd rather have liver than bread,
and liver gives him the hives.

*

So I compensate, serve him cookies,
cookies with yeast added for flavor.
It has gotten to where I even season
the beef, and Tommy, thinking it some
secret recipe, entered my meatloaf
in the company bake-off. First place
and still I'm not satisfied.
As I sit here eating my third bowl
of yeast-fortified ice cream,
I think maybe Blue Bell has something
with real shortcake in the Strawberries 'n Cream.
But then I remember that *Enquirer* article:
"Smells Can Make You Fatter—The More
You Salivate, the More You Digest!"
Used to be he called me his sweet roll.
If only he worked for Folgers
or Mrs. Paul's Frozen Fillets.
And the worst of it all, that night
I broke down and bought Hot Roll Mix
from the Seven-Eleven, to have it taste
like plain saltines. And the Wonder
I went back for, I couldn't smell.

FRIDAY NIGHTS ON THE FLOOR

When you're weaned on Coke and pasta between rushes, you learn how to wait and run right away. Being a Boffa in Boffa's Italiano and floor manager, everyone—customers, help, and family—watches you. They say restauranting's in the blood, second nature.

Fridays are the busiest. Early on, like six, people trickle in. You think you're manned okay—waters made, lemons cut, silver rolled—like maybe you won't need the extra tables Boffa brought in from the back. But when the juke starts and drops four or five nonstop, it's off and going, and in minutes, the line for seats goes out the door.

The new help thinks, Such numbers at once, it's not normal. What, did a baseball game just end? But Fridays are like that and before you know, the place is packed—talking, smoking, pepperoni pizza cooking. There's never enough room, even if you turn tables over every forty-five minutes.

You got to keep the people moving. And seat, bus, or check, you got to smile. Smiles go a long way for soothing. You can have twenty people waiting and a busser too slow to stop quick, but if you grin like God is with you, the people think, Hey, this place runs smooth.

Sometimes it takes more to please people, so you play the clapping music, E-14 or S-18 on the box. It's funny, waltzing between orders. Once they had can-can, but mostly it doesn't get faster than trot.

You always got to watch out, be prepared. Kids can be cute, but babies, they got no place. Clean up after a couple once, and you know to put them behind poles. It's their mommas really. They expect hand and feet for consommé and crackers, then leave no tip, or take their husband's.

Wrecker drivers you go slow with. They come in gritty, fingernails and all, then order two, while looking at your breasts, beer. You take maybe fifteen minutes and deliver flat. Boffa calls it crowd control. Blacks are as good as whites. Maybe LOLs are worse for sitting around. If you want to see stealing, watch them secretaries pocket sugar. Sweet and Low, it's all the same.

Some things you learn harder than others. Look at the cup and you'll spill the coffee. Put the money in the register before making change and lawyers in three-piece suits will say they gave you a twenty for a ten. The sign for choking is a hand at the throat.

About two hours into the rush, people you don't remember which table raise, Miss, Miss, could we have more water? Could we change our order? Do you have doggie bags? Where's the little-boys' room? You only have one high chair? Everything hits you—the people, the noise, the food, the used food. You take a swallow from your Coke behind the counter then see two shades of lipstick on the rim.

Boffa starts hollering at one of your waitresses. Goddamned sons of bitches, using napkins to dry silver. Where the hell do you think money comes from, the cash register? She cries and he waves a finger at you. That's one mistake. A missing ravioli makes two.

Sometimes you know Boffa's going to crap, like when you hear glass on the floor then silence. People stare out the busser and laugh—somebody's going to get it. You pick up a rag to help, but Boffa's there from behind and seethes, whispering, Don't just stand there, get a mop. With broken plates, he jingles his pocket change.

The third time around on the songs, you know it's getting near, but you can't think of sign time yet. It's easy to lose a finger to a lemon knife. Talk about smarts, they cut the same.

Five minutes of, you still got a full house, but take a breather anyway—sit with a fresh drink and eat mistakes. A waitress points out spaghetti sauce beneath your apron. If it dries more than twenty minutes, it stains the color of blood.

Even after the closing, there is the cleaning. Each tile one foot, tables are arm lengths. You wipe your face with the bandanna around your throat then retie it looser. Even after the closing there is Boffa at home. You think, Such passion the man has, it's not normal. What, should you be dying? But Boffa is like that, calls it experience. And there is the next day and the next, and Friday nights. You have to manage.

PYROKINESIS

for Paul

At first I thought of *Gaslight*,
someone pulling the wool over my eyes.
That the bushes burst into flames
the moment I looked down on them
just does not happen to the man in charge
of laser spectroscopy. I thought, Well,
it's a trick, but then no one came,
and the fire very nearly spread to the lab
before I could call someone to put it out.
Afterward, it seemed so logical,
a simple oversight; someone,
and I've seen them do this,
obviously threw their butt into the dry hedges.
But oversight or not, my colleagues
kept congratulating me on my keen reactions,
and I felt compelled to tell them
the crazy way I saw it all happen.
But later, at a friend's for the basketball
play-offs (I had set my sights on Houston
since early in the season), when he left

*

me alone with the TV while he looked
for more beer, the picture tube blew up
with three minutes left and the score
tied at 58. Houston lost and bits
of smoke even reached the smoke alarm.
His joke about the look of love
made me realize it was time I looked elsewhere,
there being more to this than meets
an ophthamologist. And calling it burnout
or stress, the Crisis Hotline people
referred me sight unseen to the head
of psychiatry at the local medical school.
Anyway, he stared me straight in the eye
and said, Maybe I've been looking
at the world through rose-colored glasses,
all is not as pleasant as first seems.
Not a minute later, he got this phone call
that his house was burning down.
But despite this "coincidence," as he called it,
and despite that, the very next visit,
he noticed a burn hole the size of a laser
beam on the leather wall behind him,
he insisted upon seeing me through all this.
And as much as I want to set my sights
on him, see things rationally again,
I worry that if I look at myself hard enough,
if I reflect too long on my condition,
I might spontaneously combust.
That must be what happened to the real people
on "That's Incredible" that my colleagues keep
kidding me about. All the world knows
of them is that their clothes remained.
I mean they could have been thinking
about another theory of relativity

*

or applying quantum physics to the intensity
of an insight. And, since the possibility
exists that these people did just spontaneously
combust, I now time all my thoughts
so as not to dwell on anything
accidentally. The hardest part is
not daydreaming, when I want to think
about my birthday or something.
Sometimes, I imagine that I know
the true meaning of a private eye.

I PICK OUT CLOTHES
FOR MY MOTHER

Possibly (1) a yellow batiste blouse
    and (2) a green, blue, and plaid skirt.
Sometimes it takes hours of digging through
    remnants
to find one piece that is hers,
the fire having leveled everything.
She cannot bear it any longer and tells me
    of (3) Italian gloves softer than skin,
        still stored in their box,
        (4) porcelain plates from China to be hidden
            until Christmas,
        (5) how my brother's return home means
            a good year.
Our minds are not the same anymore,
but in the back of mine, I know what to look for:
        (6) a teacher at a durable girls' school,
        (7) an arranger of a traveling Unitarian
            orchestra,
        (8) a master of history,
        (9) a woman of means.

*

And carefully,
protecting my hands against the elements,
I pick up whatever probable, possibly
      (10) a cashmere wrap,
whatever can be accounted for, possibly
      (11) ten assorted shoes,
or kept as sentimental,
      (12) a trailing wedding gown.
I pack it all into boxes, bags,
whatever can be containable,
then take it over to the warehouse
below where she is staying these days.
I think if I could wrap it better,
not have her see me
carry in case after case of such vulgar liquor
and meaningless detergents,
I would feel better about this Christmas.
As she watches me from upstairs
(on the twelfth day of Christmas my true love),
I think that if I bring more of her home,
if I show her some supple skin,
she would not condense
   into (13) the angora she has worn since the fire.
As I watch her now, I think
      (14) how easily she disappears behind
         each breath of air,
      (15) how delicately I must handle the china.

NEGOTIATED SETTLEMENTS AND IMMEDIATE WITHDRAWALS

The Live Eye wonders about the money,
a man holding hostages downtown wanting only
a helicopter, one thousand eighty dollars,
and a home in the Heights. However, negotiations
have broken down, and the man is tying up traffic.
And the Live Eye does not wonder how, last night,
across town, a shopping woman slapped her son
and told him she wouldn't pay two hundred ten
for him if he didn't shut up. And it does not
catch the humor in the house: the Heights
being even lower on the level of neighborhoods
than my parents', and their house being burnt up.

Even on camera, the wife will not talk to him,
recounts instead the unfortunate addresses of history:
his first suicide attempt in the hallway after Nam,
the birth of their fifth son at Methodist, his sister's
coming out in the guest room last Christmas,
how he could not afford the psychiatrist in the tower,
how they had been doing well until the burglars

*

took everything from their about-to-be-foreclosed
and sexless home. She must know the degree to which
my mother has recorded our lives, determined not to
repeat them. She knows how her husband really doesn't want
to go anywhere, home being an impossible place.

The anchor woman, stalling for reports of a settlement,
promises more details as they break. My father breaks
my routine, calls me up between a commercial
and the weather, partly cloudy high near fifty,
as I am deciding what as in whether to go to work
today or back to bed. I am sick. He says my mother
won't sleep if he rebuilds the house: she wants
a condo. I know: at least five or six stories high,
above crime, accessible only by the longest fire ladders.
He says maybe if I could talk with her again, explain
the economy, she would understand. And not wanting to,
I say, I don't think she'll listen.

I turn off the TV: the Ask the Expert man saying
we are all to blame, and the officials calling for other
family and friends. I am tired. Explaining the interest
rate to my mother has nothing to do with getting away
from it all, with how the wife knows that leaving home
means leaving forever, becoming overloaded,
having to remember even the smallest details, and connecting
a city in the palm of one hand with three souls
in the other like a couple of loose live wires.
I understand how leaving the house means putting a gun
to your head and discharging, having to kill yourself
or someone else, the world seeming never to stop itself.

SUMMER RESORT

When most of the sun goes behind Dundee,
the people point at the mountain
and call it dinner. Then, in the leftover light,
they ski once more around the lake as custom,
and the last-person-to-dry winner
gets to put up the outboard and gear.
After six it is illegal to leave a wake,
and the water sounds of fish frying, family,
and crickets. It could be nineteen forty-four here—
all eating is done campfire, by the lake.
The old lager men tell of the wicked
twelve o'clock Charlie fish that raids bait,
hook and pole, and is larger than my father's
war-record walleye hanging in the bar at Mr. Ed's.
Later, while the other kids string out tackle
and wait in their red- and green-light boats,
my brothers and I loose into the lake
the nightcrawlers we grew in sheds.

DEXTERITY

It speaks to you—the fairness of the hair.
Exaggerate orange or lemon yellow.
And beyond the head, the brush almost slipped
from my fingers, but knowing exactly what I wanted.
Instead of ordinary wall in the mean room,
infinity—a plain background of the richest blues
so the combination, bright head illuminated,
acquires mystery like a star in the depths of sky.
But this is no talent. I've sat here before,
painting the brush in my hand and my hand
without the brush. I should be better.
Imagine portraits that would appear
after a century as apparitions to the people
living then. The expression in our modern heads,
and passion, like a waiting as well as a growth.
I should try myself like Dickens or Voltaire,
but my hand cannot leave details like the storm
working over the garden in the corner.

Even in winter when ice keeps me from the fields,
frozen paint, my hands must remember the cypress
and know exactly the vertigo of corn in the North wind.
Crows fly unruffled no matter the trouble,
but still, or sleeping, I must know.
And stars ripple light across the sky as fountains
drop water onto water. The Japanese know how
it is done. Clean, clear-cut, and simple.
But these women of the South, especially
the baker's sister who touched me accidentally
as a customer, I am just beginning to see
the beauty of their breasts. The tone of the flesh
rather than the shape. To make a picture really
of the Spirit, the hand must know better than the eye.
Weavers and basket makers often spend whole seasons
alone, or almost alone, with their hands
for their only distraction. The domestic
familiar feeling keeps them going.

I have considered children, but for my part,
it is my duty to make money from my work.
If only painting were like having children—
the pain and distraction of it all would grow
less wretched. I have no trouble expressing
the loneliness of a Copperfield. Every day
I take the remedy Dickens prescribes against suicide:
a glass of wine, a piece of bread, some cheese,
and a pipe of tobacco. It is not always pleasant.
My friend Gauguin has everything: children and painting
and furniture. As far as having a wife of my own,
the more old, ugly, and ill I get, the more I want
to take my revenge by producing a brilliant color,
well arranged and resplendent. Jewelers, too,
get old and ugly before they learn how to arrange
their precious stones.

But the hand is slower than the eye and cannot
keep up with the scenery. It still scratches
the lice on the beard I shaved off three portraits ago.
Without the mirror, I don't always remember.
That morning I tried to touch the sound of bees
in Gachet's dead elm, I put my head to the bark,
forgetting again the cutting sting of it all.
There is so much to do. Even before breakfast
is coffee from old grounds, the stars pass—
night not waiting for me to see what color
I've picked up for dark. That sister's touch,
in forget-me-not blue, is lost to me forever
like a dark reflection, only the tone is remembered.
To think that Millet wept when he started painting
that Something on High, that Giotto and Angelico
painted on their knees, and Delacroix, so full
of grief and feeling, nearly smiling. . . .
What am I to be acting like this already?
These fits, I should handle myself better.
The doctors always say paint more, and always,
I want to paint more. Just today I have
three big canvases. But still, I do not know
myself in a child and need more paint
waiting for this recognition.

PATIENCE MUFFET

I won't go back in that house,
they are everywhere there,
in closets, sofas, coat pockets,
in my bed, everywhere.
They crawl on me nights,
dancing chills into my spine
like loose hair under the collar.
They drop down from rafters,
straight gossamer lines onto my
head and shoulders,
and when I eat, they are there,
surprises at the bottom of my bowl
or floating in whey.

They are everywhere,
but they don't come in through windows
like regular bugs. Father brings them in.
He hunts them with nets and tweezers,
and at night with lanterns,
because their eyes glow silver in the light

*

then go blind like morning webs
as they dew, glisten, then fade.

He brings them home. Father,
the physician who gentles people
in the front room. Father,
and he keeps spiders.
He entomologizes them,
cultivates and crosses them
to produce that ultimate fiber,
silk without silkworms, silk.

At first he only collected webs,
wrapping them on spools to wind later
around wounds. And he would instruct me.
Patience child, bandage.
Silk makes the best dressing, absorbs blood.
But the spiders intrigued him.
Patience child, look.
They have eight eyes.
And he started to study them live.
Patience child, feel.
They shed their skins once or twice a year.

And finally, he started to breed them.
Patience child, patience.
Males die soon after mating.
But new ones arrive. They are born.
They are brought in. They are all over.
And he calls me Little Miss Patience now
because I won't go back in that house.

II

MIAMI

Miami's neighbors are calling her outside.
It's six A.M. on a Sunday morning,
but Miami puts on her pink robe to go see,
the mother and father calling her all over
the complex. But as soon as they see her,
they run back inside their apartment
as they did last Thursday,
when she was wearing her Cable-TV-Ercise shorts,
her flabby legs not yet thin enough
to join the tight women who work out
at Venus de Milo. Later she thinks
she hears her name again, but it's only a cat
on her window, a black-and-white cat
that walks right in when she opens the door.
At the same time, Bill from the other side
opens his door, and she asks him
if it's his cat. He laughs no,
he's on his way to work, and laughs again,
her pink robe coming slightly undone.
She thinks the stories have started again,

*

she'll have to move. And she picks up
the cat to give it some milk but notices
Miami on its collar and drops it
to the floor with a huff. If they had asked
her if she had a brother named Orlando
or if she was, by chance, born in Florida,
she could understand. Once, while manicuring
an analyst, she was asked if her mother
had been trying to transfer herself:
My-am-I, Me-am-I, My friend-I, My daughter-I.
And not knowing what the move to Texas
had to do with it, she put the perfumed
moisturizer on his hands and said,
Miami was where her parents met on her father's leave.
The cat jumps on the sofa and falls asleep,
and Miami wonders what the shrink would say
about her neighbor's naming. At least
she wasn't named Sunny Luna or Cuba,
like the friend of a friend of a friend
born before Castro. She pokes the cat,
says, Well Miss Miami 1984, what has happened
to your looks, at least you have such a pretty face.
And she strokes it, soothsaying, You will spend
three of your lives running away from your name,
two settling down, getting married and getting fat,
two more getting divorced and cutting hair,
and the rest just trying to recover.
Then she throws it outside.
That evening, going shopping, she sees
its eyes in her headlights then watches
as it darts across the street
into oncoming traffic. Her neighbors call
her name all the way to Rosslyn and Lido.

THE TAKING OFF OF NIGHTGOWNS AND THE REMOVING OF BANDAGES

Miami's fever will break this morning.
The cat moved from her side
to bathe in the window beam and purr:
I am your sunshine, your only sunshine.
Miami kicks off the top blanket
and calls him back: *If you were Jesse,
if you were Jesse.* But she remembers
that word for people who want animals,
and worries. She cannot be one of them
although on TV they showed
"animal lovers" giving dogs
to needy kids once. Maybe it was the itch
of sweat that made her kick off
the second blanket and cough like a baker.
Mr. Zamora, the baker from Nicaragua,
would cough every time she tried
to stop the needing he said was
from the oven and poor ventilation.
He would leave her mother, bakers
sleep at odd hours, and cough,
sick people need aspirin and syrup and sleep.
Her mother liked the name Managua
and sang it like Chiquita Banana:
I'm Managua Nicaragua and I'm here to say.

*

For a moment Miami hears her husband Jesse,
but it is only a radio passing
12:30 and sunny in the city.
At 12:30 it will be three weeks,
but the first day work hasn't called.
If they've stopped calling, she can face
that concern and slips from under
the last blanket, her grandmother's
quilt. Wondering how she feels,
Miami runs her fingers over the stitches,
searching for signs of fever.
Mattresses hold secrets only as long
as the springs, but quilts recover
generations of misgivings.
Was that a lump from her mother's lover?
Did her grandfather really die in bed?
She felt only one indentation
in the place of her breast.
Last Wednesday a woman was almost raped,
but when the man saw her only breast,
he became soft and ran off crying.
The scar is so bad that Miami no longer
undresses in the bathroom. The taking off
of nightgowns and the removing of bandages
like the peeling of skin or the giving
of blood and the sickness that she cannot face
in a rush. The friends rushing, all wanting
her to go on with the names of doctors,
no longer call her. And today in the silence,
she thinks back to Jesse before the surgery,
before the divorce, to when he came back
home from that woman for the first time.
If he comes back home now, she soothes
the cat, he cannot have her dressed.

LIVING GLOVES

Miami lies to women in waiting,
especially to women in grocery stores.
Never mind that she hates coffee,
the real Mrs. Olsen is the sister
of her mother's best friend.
People, all too proper to check things out,
blush at the detail of her mother
confined to the nursing home.
Because Miami once told a nosy Safeway
checker that the six pairs of Living Gloves
were for her children's school play,
she cannot go back there without purchasing
a carton of Kool-Pops in the summer,
or lunch-box-sized assorted chips for snacks,
or without remembering to wear the birthstone
and silhouette bracelet she found
on the curb at the cafeteria.
So convenient to have engraved children.
More convenient to speak only with strangers.
She has tried to stop. For a while,

*

after the surgery, she spoke only the truth,
picking out those ladies with frivolous
blouses or those men buying feminine deodorants,
so that in asking them how they were doing,
she could return their replies with, "As well
as can be expected after major surgery,"
or "Happy to have survived the cancer."
But Miami found their shock so wonderful
that she took to starting the hibachi just
for the smell then running to Penney's or Foley's
or Frederick's of Hollywood to buy underwear,
telling everyone along the way of the fire
and how the clothes on her back weren't even hers.
Of course, having lived through a fire
as a child, she had every right,
and could produce smoldered pictures
of her fortunate aunt and uncle's wedding.
But ever since a man told her that her husband,
who by this time had died of smoke inhalation,
would not need to be embalmed—the combination
of smoke, skin, and digested food preservatives
creating a processed effect and allowing
some financial leeway—Miami has gone back
to regular lies now. Sometimes she worries
that there is a lump in her other breast
and that the sour-cream dips will outlast her.
Instead of crying, she has begun telling
all the people buying fish that they must
breathe deeply while touching, long enough
to remove all the little bones before swallowing.

BEARING

Miami's dream will end this morning.
A dose of radiation will sterilize her body,
a hot flash today, tomorrow, for five weeks,
until she's all burned out, old enough
to be her own mother. They tell her to expect
a little nausea a little like morning sickness,
being a woman she should understand.
But Miami cries, the tumor itself
among the only things she can bear
outright anymore. She had always wanted
children, Jesse saying from the beginning
a couple sons and daughters would do
him proud, and her mother always
egging them on, repeating the family
that prays together stays together,
and reminding her of how,
when Miami was just born,
an angel rested on her wondrous head
and announced that she would bear
a baby boy amidst much confusion.

*

Father Marquez, whose favorite advice
is bear and forbear, also believed
in the validity of miracles and frequently
testified on behalf of her angel,
he himself having been in the next room,
the lights suddenly surging
as if given the power from above.
And Miami remembers that on bright days
or while shopping past rows and rows
of baby blue bonnets and booties and blankets,
she would find herself wanting
to believe them, but her mother,
having been put up for adoption
at an early age, had also claimed
to be Gene Autry's rightful but secret daughter,
some men even to this day
supposedly spying on them,
and Father Marquez had also claimed
to see the image of Jesus crying
in Mrs. Delgatto's tablecloth.
But there were never any children,
Miami finding out only later,
after her second missed period,
that it was a cyst,
the doctor saying it happens sometimes
and Father Marquez telling her
don't be too quick to count the chickens,
time is a great healer,
and God works in mysterious ways.
Shortly thereafter, the doctor said
there would never be any children,
Jesse's count being unbelievably low,
and Miami took to taking only showers,
her mother convinced about throwing

*

the baby out with the bathwater.
Then, when she missed yet another period,
Jesse called her a cunt,
low-down and sleeping around,
and punched her out, her neighbor Judy
having to call the police.
Miami remembers becoming hysterical,
no one believing she took her marriage
seriously, and the shelter woman
slipping her the number of Planned Parenthood
on the side, some women able to conceive
whenever they want. Her mother wanted
a movie of the baby
and told the father it would be perfect,
Miami being (and this was news to her)
really John Wayne's daughter,
the big man sick in California
and in need of a miracle.
But there was never any movie,
the big man dying the next week,
and there was never any pregnancy,
just no more periods,
and now, as she lies down
on the table, committing herself
to the miracle of modern radiation,
Miami laughs uncontrollably
and remembers telling them all along,
the age of miracles is past.

VACATIONS AND JUSTIFIABLE CAUSES

Miami's face has lost its color.
Her doctor, for whom everything happens
easily, recommended a vacation.
Miami remembers Wanda's wedding in Wisconsin:
the Kettle Moraine was so green,
several people that spring thought
they had migraines: the white dress
looking really red in the sunshine.
But, she wonders, what happens to the color
of skin? Once, in a romance, a bikini woman
looked light green in the complex pool,
her rich tan phosphorescing in a grotto of night.
But that was an Italian socialite,
and Wisconsin is not a place for people
without reservations. If she can afford
tickets, then she might as well go all the way,
get a cabin on a lake and go out broad daylight
on a raft to sun. But, she thinks,
if she goes out broad daylight,
what will the other women say? And what

*

if the bugs think her white ears
are flowers? She could lose her hearing
like Wanda, too embarrassed to report the fly
on her honeymoon. And what if she never
came home, stayed to sun all summer
and got skin cancer? If she can afford that,
she thinks, she might as well start smoking
and eat whole dairy products,
the fats contributing to her cholesterol.
Then, Miami thinks, the rad tech taking pictures
of her now would have reason to look
like it's more than anemia and ask
if she has plans to see Paris this fall.
And everyone could point to a justifiable
cause for her headaches. And, maybe,
she could get some sleep.

MASH

Miami is scattered all over the city.
She dreams from her bed in the ward
that she is high enough to see
her watch remaining forgotten
at some repair shop, and the jeweler,
now tired of trying to locate her,
has decided to let it wind down,
the stroke of midnight but coming oddly,
like the B bed's last seizure at 10:02.
She sees her vest at the cleaners,
the people at Dapper Dan's laughing
irresponsibly, it being longer than thirty
days now, and she, not able to recover,
finally understands the goods in Goodwill
and the wounds at Purple Heart.
So she fears film left at the Fotomat,
film of Christmas and Easter
and two years ago Jesse,
but unable to be claimed,
it left under some regular name

*

and she no longer recognizable,
her face like the boy's in Rexall's,
his picture posted after falling out
of the right family's photos.
And Miami feels her heart lingering
at the shop but growing weaker every day.
The temporary stylist is already cutting
her regular customers, the others
changing their attention
to more manageable problems.
And so her lungs remain in the hallway
where she was first admitted, admitting
she could no longer breathe.
And everything that needs putting
to rest peacefully, reminds her
that what she wants most in this world
is a plot of land in her name,
simple and identifiable, her father always saying
the only thing one really leaves behind is dirt.

EARTH

Evelyn's lips are on the man next door.
She had been minding her own business weeding,
and was contemplating quitting,
it being so unbearably hot outside,
and worse, her neighbors at it again,
the husband finally painting the house
but brilliant green, and the wife red,
screaming the civic club will condemn them,
cars are already stopping to stare,
and he can go to hell for all she cares,
the sun all this while searing down,
and the husband asking and asking
for another beer, but the wife refusing,
finally calling him a drunken lout,
and him getting down off the ladder
and going to hit her, and her
picking up the can of paint
in retaliation and saying, Go ahead,
make my day. Then they relived
the fight from the day before,

*

he calling her a nag, she,
him a bad father, he,
her a bitch, she,
him a . . . a man,
and then it happened:
he grabbed his chest and fell down,
and she called, Come off it man,
do you expect me to believe that,
and then, Evelyn, Evelyn, come quick.

Evelyn is pumping now on Don's chest,
but he is not responding,
and when Susie comes back
from calling the ambulance,
Evelyn tells her to run across the street
and get Andy, her arms are getting tired,
and Andy, much bigger, would be better,
but everything will be all right,
she's had CPR. Andy, a cop,
also knows what to do and takes over
pumping on the count of three,
freeing Evelyn to do nothing but breathe,
but Don is still not responding,
and Andy starts screaming at him,
Come on, come on, come on.
He tells Evelyn to slap him
in the face while she's not breathing,
and to call his name. Evelyn pats him
on the cheek and says, Don, Don,
breathe, breathe. And Andy screams at her,
Louder, harder, and Evelyn slaps him in the face
and shouts, Don, Don, come on, come on.
But Andy shouts at her, Breathe, breathe,
and then, Louder still and harder,

*

and Evelyn boxes Don in the ear
and yells, Don you damn bastard,
nobody dies on me, nobody.

Indeed Don opens his eyes and looks
at her the look just before a scream,
but then exhales a complex syllable,
and they close, his body going suddenly
limp again, and Susie losing it,
crying, For crying out loud,
and, What Don what, and then running
down the street toward the ambulance.
The paramedics administer electroshock,
but nothing happens. They shock again,
and still nothing. And again and again,
giving him injections between each time,
and again and again and again,
and Evelyn screams at them to come on,
Nobody dies from heart attacks anymore,
call in the helicopter or something.
But they shake their heads
as if they're sorry lady,
and they load him into the ambulance,
shaking their heads again,
this time at Susie, he probably
doesn't have a chance.
Then a kid from the crowd comes up
to Evelyn and asks did she know
what happened, and Evelyn rubs
her hand over her mouth,
the taste of Don's lips suddenly
being replaced by the dirt on her hands.
She says, A struggle then, a struggle.

HINDSIGHT

Evelyn's eye is blinded by a champagne cork
six minutes into New Year's Day,
just as Mira from the University was aghast
at the fact that Evelyn hadn't known enough
to say, "Jack, Jack" the last thing before midnight
then, "Bunnies, Bunnies" the first thing afterward,
as Evelyn, all smiles, was thinking
the rabbit business some private joke
between Mira and John, John an obstetrician
and all. She screams and covers her eyes,
and John and Mira scream too,
Mira right there and John the one
opening the bottle. The party laughs
for a second then reconsiders.
On the way to the hospital,
John saying all the while, Everything
will be all right and Mira, driving,
telling John to lock the doors,
Evelyn thinks this isn't happening,
she's really on her way home,

*

and it's raining cold fog outside.
Mira says, Lock Evelyn's door especially,
remember my uncle Harry,
and then takes a corner quickly,
everyone swaying like beach grass.
Evelyn thinks of falling out,
into the deep green Gulf,
going down, down, so gently down.
Indeed her grandmother is waiting for her
at the hospital and takes her hand
calmly. She has not seen her
since she was six, but now she is younger,
her grandmother that is, and more beautiful
than ever, great white hair and deep green eyes.
Evelyn does not have to admit anything
and understands there is nothing at all
between them, the dead living and living
so peacefully. But after a while,
her grandmother withdraws her hand
and says, Evelyn, Evelyn, you must open
your eye, you must see your future,
your time will come. Evelyn opens
her eyes and sees the doctor slapping her
on the face, saying, I want you
to listen to me, we're trying to save
your eye, but it will be touch and go.
Touch and go. Evelyn moans, alone again
for the greater part of her life.

UNCLE WALTER

Evelyn's uncle Walter is killed
in an electrical accident,
and she is not really upset,
her uncle having fondled her as a child,
but goes to the funeral anyway,
her aunt always seeming so frail.
At the funeral people are crying,
and Evelyn tries to sympathize,
even after hearing her cousin tell
another relative it was such a shock,
she was in the middle of lunch,
and it was a shock.
But in the middle of the testimonials,
when Evelyn checks the program
to see how much longer, she sees
the mortuary's slogan printed
at the bottom—"Never Put a Question
Mark Where God Has Put a Period"—
and has to cover her mouth and run
out of the room, barely getting beyond

*

the double doors before bursting
into laughter, the idea of God's
punctuation enough to make anyone die.
But before Evelyn can even wipe
the tears from her eyes, her cousin
also bursts into the foyer crying.
They smile at each other nervously
for a second then sob out loud,
two grown women carrying on like children.
At the reception later,
her aunt continues to mistake everything
and whispers in her ear
she never knew she cared
so much about Walter, Walter always
saying he had a special place
in his heart for her.
Evelyn thinks for a second
then says, Yes, he cared for me
just like his daughter,
there's no question about it.

LIP SERVICE

for Will 1957–1973

Evelyn's lips are on the cover of *Vogue*,
or so she imagines as she's paying for a *Life*,
she is not from the South, her lips
are not fat, and Curt had never died.
But quickly, before recounting the change,
she catches herself and draws in her smile,
the boy behind the counter saying only then
to have a nice day. Evelyn remembers
flipping through the pages of *Better Homes
and Gardens* that summer she turned
thirteen and her cousin Curt, back six months
already from Vietnam and trying
to find a job, moved in with them.
She would cut out the pictures
and create her own home, well rounded,
three bedrooms, sometimes four,
enough for several brothers and sisters.
Once while searching through her mother's
belongings for some other issues,
she came upon some adoption papers

*

and a letter from an agency,
but neither containing any clear information.
She tried to bring up the matter
that night at dinner, but Curt interrupted,
said he could tell she was from the South,
women from the South always have
such fat lips. But largely from the fact
that her parents were themselves
from Wisconsin, she had never before
considered she was from the South,
despite being born in Houston's Heights.
As her mother explained it later,
after they had had her, they had
considered adoption, and Evelyn remembers
that there were some resemblances, plenty of people
from then on pointing out exactly how much
she had both her father's and her mother's eyes,
but no one, except for her cousin,
matched her lips, and him from Alabama
and unable to land a job.

Evelyn gets on a bus with her *Life*.
The driver is broadcasting vintage Stones,
and Evelyn can't get out of her mind
the face of Mick Jagger's satisfaction,
his lips looking, as Doctor John so often jokes,
childbearing in action. Evelyn witnesses
a woman putting on lipstick up front.
She blots it dry with a Kleenex
then carefully checks the impression.
Evelyn remembers being eighteen and having
an Estée Lauder woman stop her
at a cosmetics counter and say she could
make over her face in twenty minutes,

*

diminish her lips and accentuate her eyes.
Thirty dollars later, her mother said
she looked ghastly, terrible, and Evelyn
went back to her regular self again.
A new song begins and Evelyn wonders
what John really can tell about lips
and if he makes secret marks
on his patients' charts as to whether
they are kissers or bearers or of no interest at all.
Just before Curt went off, her mother fixed him up
with the neighbor's daughter Linda,
and Linda reported some months later,
after he had done it, that she had ended
their date early because he really only wanted
to kiss her, to sit in the car and kiss her.
Still later, Evelyn remembers bringing home
her best friend Will and hearing her mother
ask them if they'd been kissing,
their faces seeming slightly puffy.
It was then she noticed his fat lips,
how much they really were related,
and by and by he quit being himself.

Evelyn finally arrives home with her *Life*,
thoroughly depressed. She catches
a glimpse of her face in the mirror
as she's changing clothes, and runs
into the kitchen, but the knife rack
also makes her feel like dying,
and she ricochets into the living room,
sees the sixth-floor view, then bounces back
again into the bedroom for some Valium.
She knows the pattern well; it's happened
before; there's no use moving about;

*

it will always get her; her day
will come. Every time she hears Will
telling her just exactly what he's going to do,
and every time she just listens, thinking
that's the only thing one can do,
her cousin having driven that point home
by way of Houston, Colorado, Sacramento, and Mobile,
and she does nothing to stop him,
her cousin having fixed his lips
by blowing away the rest of his mouth,
and she remembers over and over
that line of Will's just hanging there,
his lips still slightly blue at his funeral,
and very, very fat, the each of them
like each other, the none of them like
their parents, and she, now, still swallowing
the all of it.

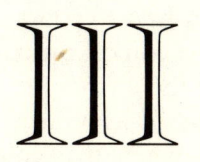

III

GEORGE

I.

It's almost laughable, your head
rolling down your arm like a basketball
and bouncing to the floor, you chasing
after it, down the stairs and out the screen.

You could lose it at any time,
out in public, as complicated
as a meteor falling out of the blue
and hitting the car next to yours
which in turn runs you off the road,
the collision with the ditch
snapping your neck at its weakest point,
C-2 through C-6, where they chipped
away bone to get at the tumor,
leaving just enough, or so they hope,
to support your head.

Or it could be as simple as a book
falling mysteriously off the stacks
and axing you squarely in the neck.

It could be a nod.

I imagine you alone in your bed,
the most dangerous place of all.
It's a bad dream when I try to hug you.

Sometimes, since you've told me
about this fear, I think it's our hope
that you lose your head. You can drive off
in your green suit then, and come back
year after year until they find a cure.

II.

The morning after the hurricane
I can't stand it anymore.
Green trees down five and six thick.
Green limbs broken all over the yard.
Green fall on the green grass.
Green leaves glued to the green house.
Green juice in the green gutters.
I can't stand it anymore
because I know right away
that the men with the chain saws
will return as they did after the tornado,
and night and day they'll cut up
the trees, one by one, bit by bit,
until there are no more in the road,
no more on the cars and boats and houses,
until there's nothing left to cut
but the trees still surviving.
I can't stand it anymore
because I know they'll cut
the survivors then, one by one,
because storm by storm we've grown

*

afraid of anything that large and that green.
And soon I'll wake greener,
my hands and my face and my clothes.
I can't stand it anymore
because when I do reach a live phone,
the phones at the hospital are dead,
and I can't reach anyone
who can reach you except your parents
who can't come to the phone
because they're out in the garage,
deciding whether to kill a green snake.
I sit down in the booth,
green leaves glued to the green glass,
and I put my hands on my ears,
green hands on the green face,
and I storm out loud:
One two three four.
Testing one two three four.
Hello, my name is Lynn.
Six seven eight nine ten.
I have two hands attached to two arms
attached to my shoulders
attached to my neck to your neck
to this neck I don't know where.
And silenced then, I start back
slowly to my house, realizing
it's three months to the day
from the tornado last May,
three months to the day
that your neck started hurting you again.
I can't stand it anymore
because I know that tomorrow,
when I begin to clean up the green,
the whole city will have betrayed you.

III.

After your third surgery,
I bring you *5001 Nights at the Movies,*
and you break its spine loudly,
almost laughing with pleasure.
I laugh too, but ambiguously,
half the laugh of a fraud discovered,
half the laugh of a confessor relieved.
We laugh together then, out loud,
and for the first time,
I understand the rules of the game.
I will have the life you hunt for
and carry it on with the people
you leave behind.
I will go to the ends of the earth
living on, living testament
to your powers of regeneration.

NECK AND NECK AND NECK OR NOTHING

To be stiff-necked is to have
radiation change the shape of your spine;
to stick your neck out is to have a neck
so weak from surgery it can't hold
the head upright; *to break your neck*
has nothing to do with effort exerted.

I'm lost without the idiom.
Back in East Texas used to be
you were born *neck-ed* and went mad *neck-ed*.
Further west, *necking* is on the ranch,
tying a restless animal to a tame one,
making them both tractable.

But this business with the neck
places you halfway in the underworld
and looking back. I'm thinking of *necrosis* now,
the way your heart is taking the chemo.
I want to call in a medium, a *necromancer*
to help us regain our direction.

Then there are always the questions:
What was the *nectar* of the gods? Who is calling
this race? And for what purpose are we running?
It's not that we long to say *I'm so happy
I could die,* but that we can say
the word *cancer* and excel.

THE EMBARRASSMENT

We know this to be true. You will undergo
an embarrassment, an embarrassment
for which you will die a small death,
and I, I will have to let go your hand
to join the people from all around
who will come to stare at you.
If it were any lesser matter,
I would simply behave as you,
follow your lead, drop my fork on my plate,
say Yes, yes I believe in miracles,
I believe in the pearly gates,
we will be together always.
Perhaps that is what should happen:
I, I will keep hold of your hand,
and we will be brought down together,
the embarrassment again, the both of us.
But here we wait in the meantime,
the both of us breathing as if about
to be discovered, my other hand
set lightly beside your in-and-out chest
so that I might not miss it,
the most quiet of all exchanges,
the doctors in the next room
content to write "pulmonary embarrassment"
and not "cancer" as the cause of death,
and you and I here alone,
you turning blue, the both of us dying.

SCHOOL OF THE WOODS

It's 10:01 and you are breathing
regularly, twelve times a minute,
five seconds apart, these things I notice
because my mother has taught me to notice,
yellow mist rising from the body
of Ernest Wood two minutes twelve seconds
after his last breath, my mother coming
quickly in the living room to get us,
me, seven then, and my brother, eleven,
and we breathed in the air,
and we breathed out, then we breathed
again until she said it was all gone,
everyone eventually returning their attention
to the body, realizing a great thing
had passed, and me aware
for the first time of air
as if just slapped by the hand
of delivery, peculiar and compelling,
this exchange of life;
with every breath since I've wondered
how much of the genius remains
within me, and what does it all mean,
the kindly Mr. Wood leaving life like that,
just hours after finishing a book,
and why am I driven so,

*

thinking, thinking, forever thinking,
and what urged me to stop
at a used-book sale some twenty years later,
look for two minutes, and pick out
his last book sight unseen,
one title among millions,
one mind among billions;
I am bursting with energy and with pain,
never able to control
the mingling of life and death,
feeling beyond old and most miserably
imprisoned yet wet in my youth
and gushing for the sake of gushing,
this odd paradox, the parable
of my existence, and the arc in between,
the pinnacle of my discrimination:
Oh I am lost, Oh I am found,
Oh I am here, Oh I am there,
Oh I am everyone and no one,
all things and nothing,
yet breathing, breathing all the time,
and now sitting here next
to you here breathing,
thinking how each breath must be
at once binding to people and life unseen,
yet moving closer and closer
toward the last, my mind still impressionable
after twenty-seven years and futilely waiting
for you here on the respirator,
futilely interpreting the space between
each breath as my mother interpreted
Mr. Wood's, the rest of your body
failing more every day,
the none of us ever able, at last, to die.

WAKE UP

I want the man in our office asking about suspensions
to know that while I am in the meantime checking,
he has only thirty-six hours to live if the sun goes out,
sixteen minutes in the event of nuclear war,
240 seconds should his lungs stop breathing,
one gasp for a gunshot wound to the heart.

I want the woman who sharpens my pencils
to know that their perfect points last only long
enough to figure the stress on a bridge
for half an hour, the expanse of just one
guy wire, or the number of suicides
that will leap off its crossing in one lifetime.

And the people in the pool who complain
about the lifeless Razorbacks have no idea
of what really causes split ends, baldness,
or the speed in which great lengths fall to the ground,
or the amount of DNA in one simple strand,
and whether hair continues to grow after death.

And do the other engineers really know
what makes people go on, why some, so willing
to believe the suspension, cross
without breathing, while others believe differently,
consume each second as if it were their reactor,
drive themselves deeply into the current?

I want to make up the difference, slap people
on the back with the bulwark of our passing,
draw up the bridge if necessary to keep us
always on the edge and afraid of letting go,
as if just startled by the thought of a child,
knowing something has happened, will happen, soon.